YIN

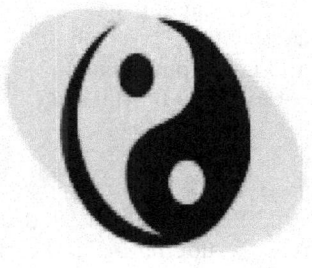

YANG

First Edition

By

Patricia Thrushart

"WHEREVER YOU GO, GO WITH ALL YOUR HEART."

~ Confucius

Quimby, Pickford & Cheshire Publishers
P.O. Box 264 Rossiter, PA 15772

Yin & Yang
First Edition, June 1, 2011
ISBN 13: 978-0-9822510-6-5 ISBN 10: 0-9822510-6-8
Library of Congress Cataloging-in-Publication Data
Library of Congress Control Number: 2009936921
Yin & Yang
\ Thrushart, Patricia

Volume discounts are available from Quimby, Pickford &
Cheshire® and the author, for counseling, outreach and
promotional purposes. The author is available for public
speaking engagements at no fee.

cover art: Yin and Yang Curtsy by Brennah Soukup

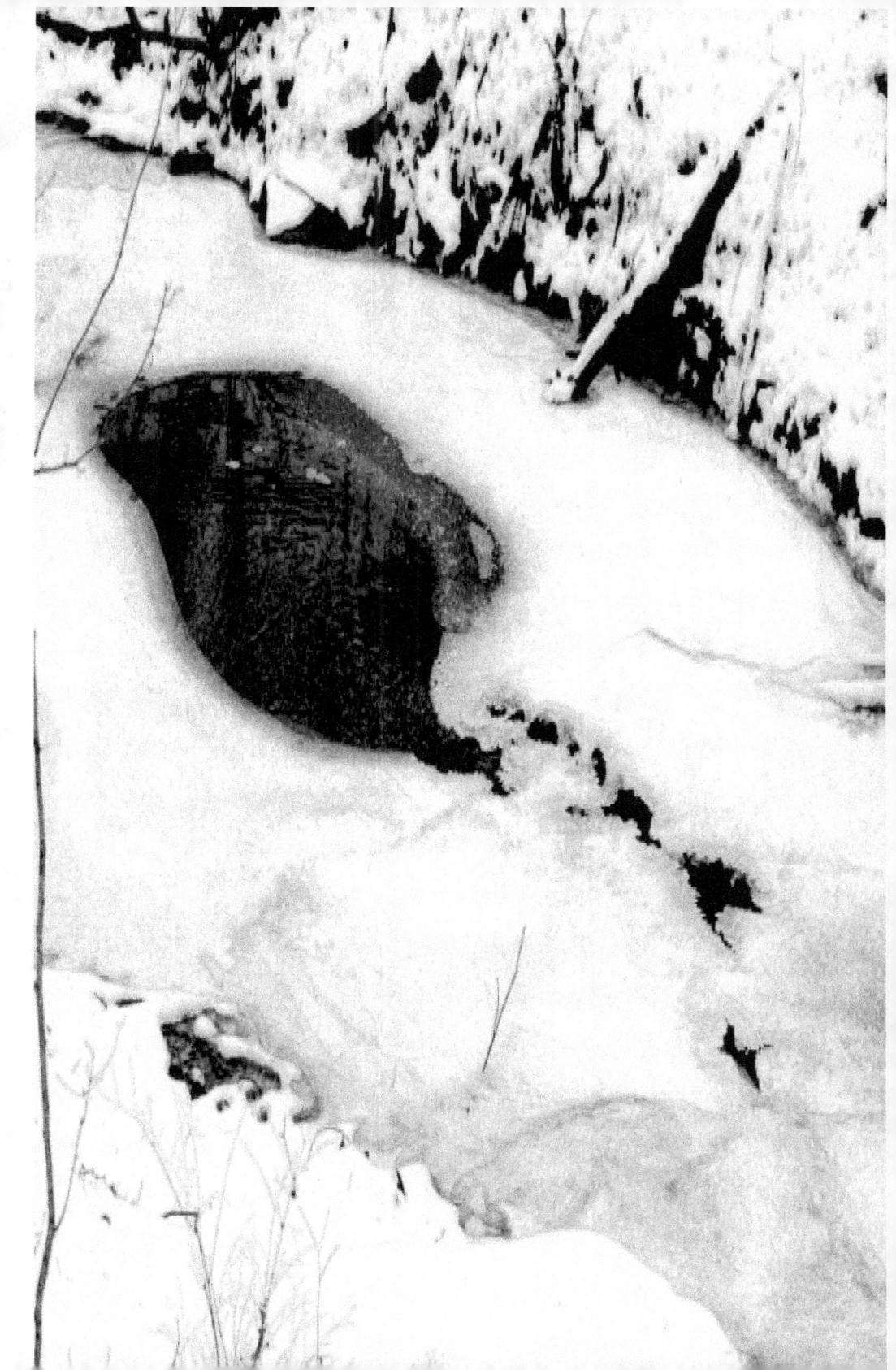

DEDICATION

For all women, that we find the balance within

ourselves.

YANG DIALOGUE   YIN DIALOGUE

Yang	Yin
I fight	*I deflect*
I take	*I give*
The Sun	*The Moon*
The Heat	*The Cool*
Hard	*Soft*
Testosterone	*Estrogen*
Man	*Woman*

TABLE OF CONTENTS

YIN & YANG
POEMS AND ESSAYS

TABLE OF CONTENTS

YIN & YANG
POEMS AND ESSAYS CONTINUED

TABLE OF CONTENTS

YIN & YANG
POEMS AND ESSAYS CONTINUED

TABLE OF CONTENTS

YIN & YANG
POEMS AND ESSAYS CONTINUED

INTRODUCTION

I never remember my dreams.

I am an early riser, and when I wake up, I rarely have the inclination to lull myself back to sleep. My mind starts buzzing with what I want to do, I get excited about the day, and before long my feet hit the floor no matter how early in the morning it is. (And personally, I can think of nothing more beautiful than a spring morning and the sound of birds as the sun rises). But recently I have been trying to put myself back to sleep when I wake up very early, especially in the cold of winter, and in doing so, have actually begun to remember some dreams. I must fall into REM sleep, and when the alarm rings, they stay fresh in my mind.

These two dreams I am about to recount were from the same morning. (If you love to interpret dreams, you should have a field day with these!)

In one, I am living in a house that is open, without doors in the doorways or glass in the windows. My daughter and one of my sisters are with me. We live in a hostile place, like Pandora in the movie Avatar, or Australia (sorry, couldn't help that— author Bill Bryson says that everything there can kill you).

So in my dream, I have to monitor where my daughter is relative to the constant dangers I see—huge crocodiles in the back yard and giant ants who rear up on their hind legs as they enter the house. But I am calm—I reach for a stove pipe that I hope is hot in order to hit a giant

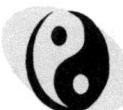

insect on its head and keep it from hurting us. At no time do I feel fear—just resolve and responsibility.

In the second dream, I have been mistakenly admitted to a clinic for young and clearly insane women. They all look alike—in their twenties, pretty, and brunette. They cannot meet my eyes; they cannot speak in coherent sentences; they are jittery and act possessed.

The clinic is run by a cultish group of equally young and pretty women, but blonde, who actually share many characteristics with their patients but are in charge. These counselors act very sweet, but beneath the surface I sense they are evil—they do not really wish for their patients to heal. They enjoy being in control.

I assess the situation and determine that I am much older than all of these women, that I will be able to demonstrate my sanity, and that I should not be here. I feel an enormous sense of calm and focus. I approach one of the counselors and introduce myself, holding out my hand. She fears a trap and will not take my hand. Instead she tries to hug me and mutters insincere words meant to soothe me. I assure her I am not ill, and engage her in calm conversation with eye contact—things the patients are unable to do. I explain that I should not be here—that it is a mistake.

She points out the tattoo on my wrist—*an inmate's number*. I insist there has been a mistake. She becomes fearful and tightens her grip on me, attempting to use physical intimidation to control me.

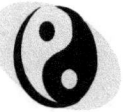

But as I have a black belt and have trained against bear hugs, I break free deliberately and with strength. I am conscious of the fact that they might use other means to restrain me, even drug me, but I feel confident that I will prevail. Then I wake up.

I am sure there are many levels of meaning in these dreams. They evoke imagery from some movies I had recently seen; they speak of my sense of responsibility for my daughter, my concern for my sister, perhaps even my awareness of my aging body. But notice this: I was in dangerous situations in both dreams, and yet I felt no fear.

This is my affirmation: with age and maturity come mental strength and confidence.

And my, that's a good thing.

For don't you think that women of "middling " years in particular have lives that can be best called hazardous balancing acts? We are often called to be both child and caregiver to our parents, mother and lover to our spouses, worker and homemaker to our families, parent and friend to our children.

Society quickly, superficially, labels us saints or whores and judges us on whether we look younger or older, if we are fat or thin, pretty or ugly, even blonde or brunette (or gray).

No other group of people is more in need of understanding the ancient concept of Yin and Yang than women of middling years. For us, an out-of-balance condition can mean mental and tactical chaos for many people in our lives.

But it is not an easy concept to fully understand, especially in a Western world. For years I studied the Korean martial art of Tang

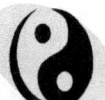

Soo Do. Three days a week, fifty-two weeks a year, and for thirteen years, I would see the Korean flag in our school while meditating, sparring, practicing.

The flag's most noticeable feature is the Yin and Yang symbol.

We studied the meaning of the flag, and I dutifully passed the oral and written tests, but to be honest I never really internalized the true meaning of the symbol at its center.

Then I happened on an amazing article—one which described the origins of Yin and Yang as an astronomical phenomenon observed by the early Chinese—and somehow this linking up of the symbol with the celestial movement of the heavens grounded the concept for me. (You can find this article on the internet if you search for it).

At the same time, much of my poetry began taking on the characteristics of a dialogue—sometimes a question and answer, other times looking at a single emotion from two different, often opposite, points of view. During this time, I was struggling with various out-of-balance conditions in my own life—with people taking more than giving, or me giving way too much and not asking for what I needed.

But like water filling a space, equilibrium does finally come to pass. It may not be at the level we planned or wanted, but it is equilibrium. Life moves back in balance because it must. And so the title of this collection of my more recent poems is a tribute to the inevitable balancing.

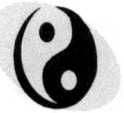

It is tribute to all women who become masters at the balancing act, and to the movement of the heavens that trace the great and ancient symbol of Yin and Yang.

Seek it. *And dream strong.*

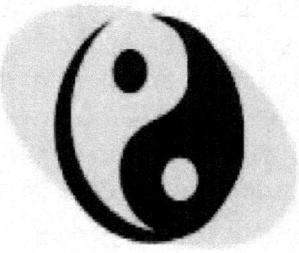

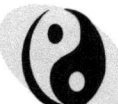

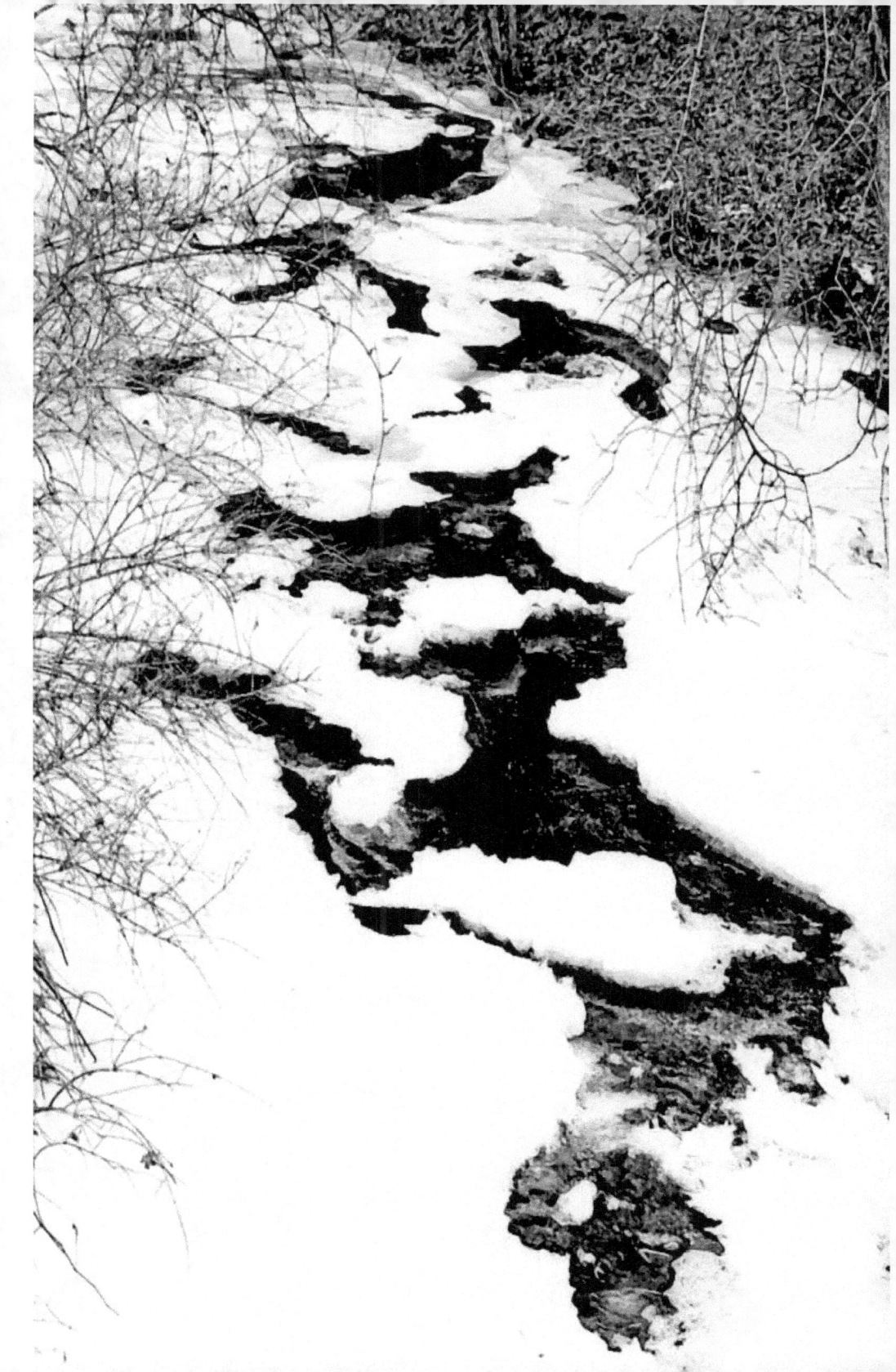

THE MEANDERING COURSE
PHOTO BY PATRICIA THRUSHART
PART OF THE STREAM SERIES

FOREWORD

"All things change, nothing is extinguished. There is nothing in the whole world that is permanent. Everything flows onward; all things are brought into being with a changing nature; the age themselves glide by in constant movement."
        —Ovid, *Metamorphoses*

"All flesh is grass, and its beauty is like the flower of the field: The grass withers, and the flower fades."
        —Isaiah 40:6

Recently I have been thinking a lot about Change and its ultimate steward, Death. These thoughts led me to write a poem called "He Moves Upon the Water" which explores the reality that Change is constant and impossible to avoid. And yet, we play fickle with it like an uncommitted lover. We embrace Change when it is kind, but bewail it when it is harsh, and even try to deny its inevitability. We earnestly wish to stay in our comfort zone— the proverbial Status Quo.

As fickle as we are with Change, we are worse with Death—especially our own. We tend to ignore it completely. Oh, intellectually each of us acknowledges that some day we will die, but surely it will be a long time from now! Then we seem to shut that part of our brain down—just as we always wake up before dying

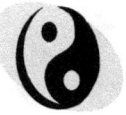

in a dream. I think the average human brain is wired in some way to compartmentalize the intellectual realization that we will die. And so we live as if we are immortal—as if we always have more time.

We persist in this attitude even if we experience a certain type of change that suggests an end far closer than we had allowed ourselves to imagine. Perhaps someone close to us receives a difficult diagnosis that comes with treatment options measuring the remainder of their life as a statistical probability. Perhaps we see images on a television screen of the human toll and physical devastation of an earthquake. We think for a moment: "There but for the grace of God go I." And then we go on as if we will live forever—putting off that reconcilement with an estranged relative. Forgetting to tell our child we love him at the end of the day. . . passing by the elderly neighbor's house without knocking on the door. After all, there is always tomorrow!

I wonder: shouldn't a diagnosis, an earthquake, the death of someone dear be enough to remind us to live each day as if we have no more time? I don't mean that we throw ourselves into risky behaviors like bungee-jumping or parachuting, or pursue that one thing we always wanted to do for ourselves before we die (a la "The Bucket List"). I am asking what changes we should make within the regular rhythm of our lives—working, parenting, neighboring, loving—because we know that someday we will die—as will our loved ones. Our death was a certainty the day we were born. A drunk driver, an Act of God, an abnormal growth of cells, could be waiting for any of us. Tomorrow.

My affirmation is to try and live each day with a more deliberate realization that what I have today will be gone tomorrow, that Change is certain, and Death is waiting. And in that realization, to be more grateful for the gifts of the Present, and the joys they bring.

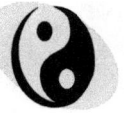

ACKNOWLEDGEMENTS

For **inspiration**, I thank: my beautiful daughter, for she amazes me with a maturity beyond her years, a wisdom sometimes beyond mine, and a fierce belief in fairness. Thanks to my wonderful son, for he enlightens me with his spiritual depth and Buddhist discipline. My past teachers of poetry, for their enthusiastic readings of the greatest English poets reverberate in my ears today. Also, I thank the volunteers, staff and clients of *Dress for Success*, for their awe-inspiring selflessness and their tactical support of women.

For **support**, I thank: My publisher, great friend, and fellow poet Girard Tournesol, without whom these books would not exist—I thank you for so many things with my whole heart. My parents, whose love becomes more evident to me every year. My sisters, who are and always will be my best friends, and my namesake Aunt and Godmother, who first taught me what complete acceptance really means.

Thank you to Kathy Carlson for her fine editorial eye and to all the people known and unknown to me who helped turn a typed document into the book you hold in your hand.

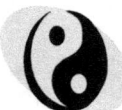

YIN & YANG
POEMS AND ESSAYS

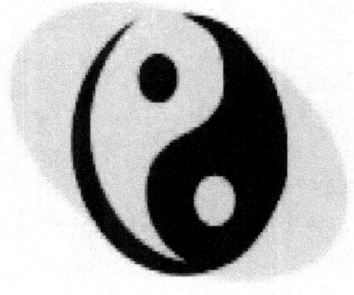

THOSE OF A CLOVEN DISPOSITION

Those of a cloven disposition—
ancestral prey of cruelty—
(a horse, perhaps, or unicorn)
will graze sweet grass uneasily
alert for vulnerability—
inelegant vulgarity,
the threat of insecurity,
separation anxiety—
and every fiber
every bone
every instinct
every honed
SENSE
will say—NOW FLEE!
Yes, you—now FLEE and HIDE—
you fool!
Do it now—protect your pride—
your sanity, serenity,
your every equanimity!
At just the hint,
at just the scent,
at just the possibility—
Those of a cloven disposition
from years of hurt mentality
will feel the urge to fly.

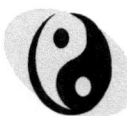

ADVICE

Step graciously from dark to sun—
Emerge a-blink from shadow dim
To light a-dazzled and a-rimmed
With promise of a fuller life—
A life that will be rich and clear
Not without risk—
Not without fear—
But tangible with laughter found
And moments seized where love abounds.
Where simple things are savored sweet
And ritual will grace each feat
Of independence, courage, trust—
Because of this, my love, you must:
The risks you'll take are YOURS to brave—
The fears you'll conquer YOURS to save
From incandescent photon beams—
The shadows cold retreating fast—
YOURS the face sun-blessed at last.

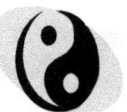

AGAINST MY EVERY
TRUE INTENTION

Against my every true intention
the words I speak
create a tension
stark and searing
sparked and arched
across the wireless stretching space
that separates two minds, two hearts,
(and whose is whose)
two halves,
too long.
Digitized and disembodied,
disconnected from the body
aching to lay down the touch
that simply explains
All.

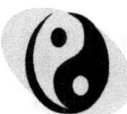

I COULD LIVE
ANYWHERE WITH YOU

I could live anywhere with you
For with you any language is
the music of my tongue
and any city a labyrinth of gifts
any house a womb
any child a god.

I could live anywhere without you
for without you every language is a noise,
every place like every other place,
every house a tomb
and every child a pang.

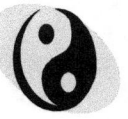

THE COURSE
OF LOVE MEANDERS

The course of Love meanders—
the Key turns on itself in pattern.
Demanding patience all the more
as Athena paces the tiled floor.
Her sandaled footsteps lightly down
to trace the geometric ground.
And mortal woman,
mortal man,
turn and twist,
revise their plans.
With each gyration,
each Reverse,
Love finds Reason more perverse.

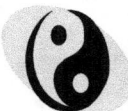

WE SAIL

We sail
across a dappled lake
a skip across the wake
awake
to every tiny breath
of breeze
and every shiver
of the sail—
alive to every shift
the boom might make—
we duck
as it swings by
and laugh each time.
We tack
as we confront the wind
that keeps us from
our destined shore.
We pull the ropes
that bind us up
and twist the rudder hard—
and jib and tip—
and shift our weight—
and skim along a blissful pace—
the promise of the
glassy lake.

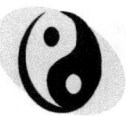

THE TROTH

I plight my troth
With cups of wine
In a valley of cedar trees
Ringed by redwoods high and old
And brushed with salty tang,
Filled with vines tangled in grapes
Among fields growing sere.

West of ancient Lebanon,
North of modern Sodom
(Flushed with cash and its cache)
The brindled cows do graze the sedge
And gaze at swales of gold.

I plight my troth
With salty skin,
Nerve on nerve,
And lips on lips
Under the sun,
Amid the vines.
The piney sap
And herbal oils
Anoint my head
And fingers.

I plight my troth
Just like a man
who clings to wife or life
Or like the lover shedding tears
When she must leave the valley's sweep
And tear from its embrace
With all the wrath of fate.

28

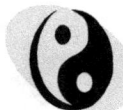

THE TROTH
CONTINUED

This troth is seared by intimacy
And grounded fast in poetry
Wedded full in brilliancy
Of spoken word and common thought.
Celebrated in a crush
Harvested by hand,
And fed on lush goats' milk and honey
While tongue and ear and eye and skin
Plight hard and long and lovely.

A covenant set like red wax,
A moment drunk like wine,
As piney sap
And herbal oils
Anoint my head
And perfume my hair
And fingers.

Napa Valley
October, 2009

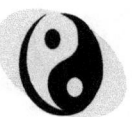

YOU SAT WITH ME BESIDE THE HEARTH

You sat with me beside the hearth
I replayed stories and for my part
remembered grade school cruelty
(the petty snivel group-think evil
of eighth-grade Catholic schoolmates).
They hated me, I'd always thought
because of weirdness I'd been taught
by long-dead authors who did write
of musty English drawing rooms
(their high cravats and tightly bound-up
manners).
Then you stepped through the door I'd opened,
The door of my own memory,
and posited another theory—
perhaps it was my Jewish name.
While I, so like the bleeding scapegoat
scarred and struck by sinners' guilt
had always thought the reason was
in ME—
striving to be loved, but unlike the lamb—
not Worthy.

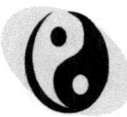

SEEKING STRENGTH

A danger lurks in seeking strength
when love is far away,
and goblins hover in the air
with face to save or bills to pay.

Strength does spring up
from deep-drawn wells
of blessed confidence—
Resolve renewed by memory's
sweet and sacred confluence.
The soul awash, the body rinsed,
the heart baptized anew.

But strength can also be propped up
by playing "what-if" as a test
that conjures sad imagined ends
and stirs up empty spoken quests—
"I will survive NO MATTER WHAT."

This self-inflicted entrancement
creates a state of detachment—
just as a moist and jeweled prey
will sacrifice a limb to save
its short and crippled life.

I guard against this danger since
detachment is a hoary frost—
it seems quite beautiful at first
in all its lace adornment,
but under each iced prickled point
is all but certain death.

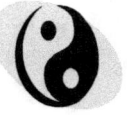

SYMPATHY STRINGS

We are tuned in precise sympathy
like sitar strings—

    Those outside tangible, thick and strong.
     Those inside too delicate to touch.

The first we pluck with the inadequacy of words
and grudgingly they drone
heavy in the languid air between us.

But suddenly
the small slender sympathy strings stir
shiver
shimmer
vibrate to sweet life
trembling with resonance
with pureness
with clear delight
until
(impossible to touch)
they sing.

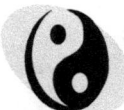

THE HEART OF A HUMAN
BEING IS NO DIFFERENT
FROM THE SOUL OF HEAVEN
AND EARTH. IN YOUR LIFE,
ALWAYS KEEP IN YOUR
THOUGHTS THE INTERACTION
OF HEAVEN AND EARTH,
WATER AND FIRE, YIN AND
YANG.

~ Morihei Ueshiba

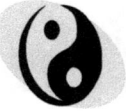

THE GREAT GIFT

"Walk away quietly in any direction and taste the freedom of the mountaineer. Camp out among the grasses and gentians of glacial meadows, in craggy garden nooks full of nature's darlings. Climb the mountains and get their good tidings, Nature's peace will flow into you as sunshine flows into trees. The winds will blow their own freshness into you and the storms their energy, while cares will drop off like autumn leaves. As age comes on, one source of enjoyment after another is closed, but nature's sources never fail."

—John Muir
Our National Parks, 1901

"I went to the woods because I wished to live deliberately, to front only the essential facts of life, and see if I could not learn what it had to teach, and not, when I came to die, discover that I had not lived."

—Henry David Thoreau
Walden, 1854

      When I was a teen-aged girl in the throes of hormonal changes, low self-esteem and confusion, I sought solace in hiking, singing and reading. A camp counselor, who I thought of as a grown and wise woman, but who was probably only eighteen herself, introduced me to the writings of Henry David Thoreau. I was fourteen. It was then that the sense of peace and fullness that I experienced while in the

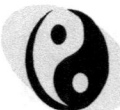

woods became articulated— a philosophy, not just my preference! A movement, not just a teen-aged girl's quirk! I was a pantheist!

Thoreau led me to Emerson, Emerson led me to Muir, and Muir led me to appreciate, and desire to visit, the great Parks of our country. (And to the Sierra Club!)

What a great gift and legacy we Americans have in our National and State Parks system. What a travesty to see their funding eroded and future uncertain! We take for granted the ability to call an office or visit a website, search for a date and reserve a camp site or cabin for a small fee, arrive at the designated time to a place surrounded by incredible natural beauty, pitch a tent and start a fire— *as if the place belonged to us.* And it does. Imagine the cost of buying that land ourselves for the few times we would use it; imagine the loss if that land were privately owned and not available to us otherwise.

Without access to these places, we would lose so much— to see the sky from a dark place and understand why the Milky Way is so named; to hear nothing mechanical mask the songs of birds or frogs; to feel our ears ache from silence (and allow us to hear our own thoughts); to smell loam, or lake or lichen; to see nothing concrete; to taste the scent of fire.

Weather matters not; I have nestled in a warm cabin in three foot of snow after cross-country skiing; I have slept to the lullaby of rain on the roof a tent; I have cooled off in a running stream after hiking in the heat. Every season and every storm brings beauty in the woods.

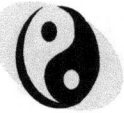

I meet up with myself in the woods, without the distractions of city, school, museum. I have visited great cities in Europe and America and will do so again— but in cities my focus is outward— the image I project, the stimuli around me, the noise, energy, pace. In the woods my focus is inward. A fortunate life enjoys a balance of both.

I never enter or leave the woods without writing a poem; there is an immediate surge of emotion and marvel when I am fortunate enough to spend time somewhere beautiful. A hill, a mountain, a bird, a deer become symbols and protagonists in my writing. I am most prolific when tucked away at a "stay-cation."

The poems in this book that I wrote while at the lovely Ohio State Park called Deer Creek are a testimony to the joy of these places and the solace they offer. I hope to see you there someday—we'll pass on a wood-chip trail along a ridge above a sparkling lake. We'll nod and smile, lost in our own thoughts and mindful of the singing thrush.

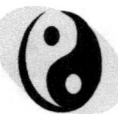

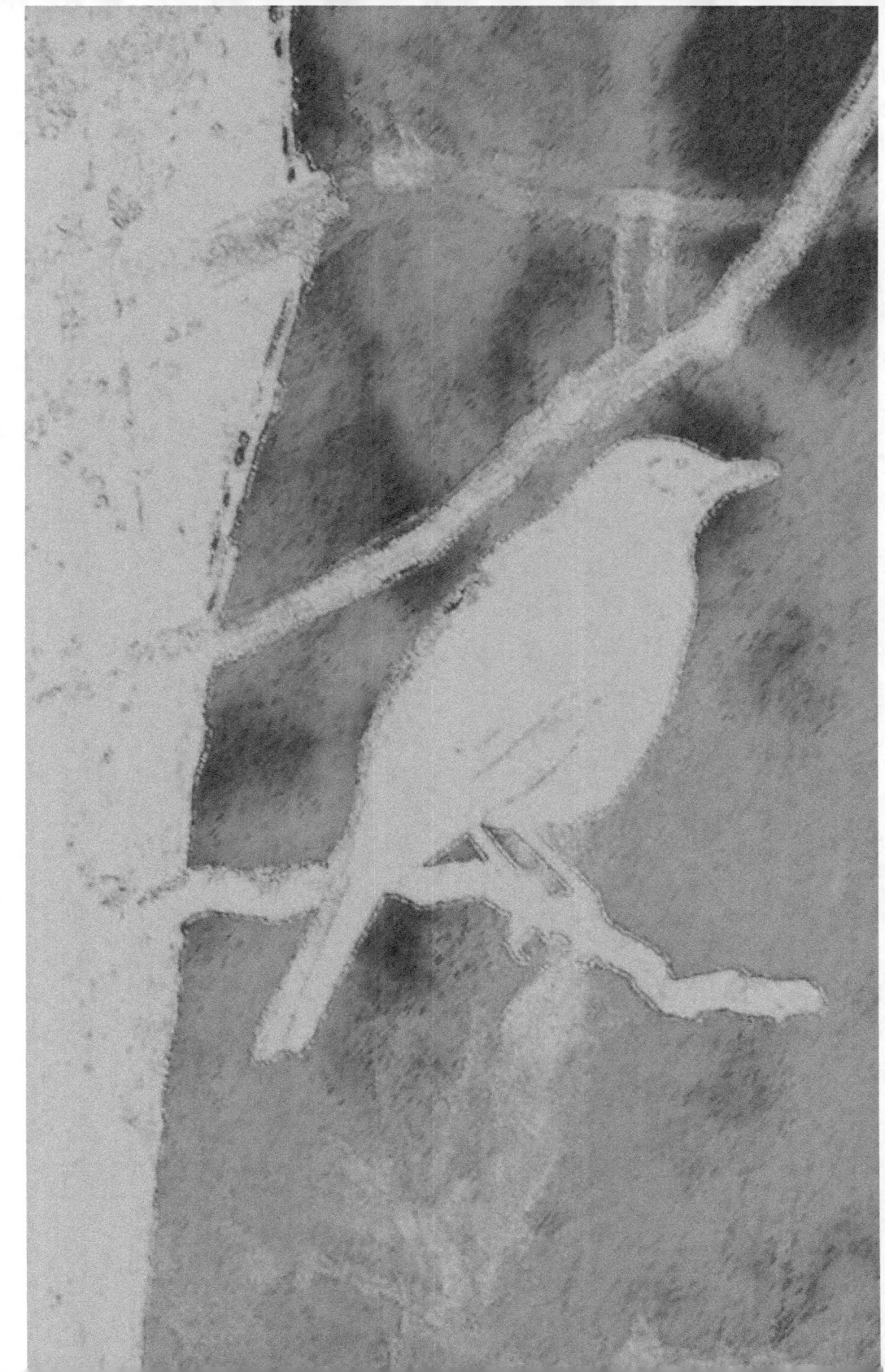

THE SINGING THRUSH
PHOTO BY PATRICIA THRUSHART
PART OF THE DEER CREEK SERIES

LUNA MOTH
(NEARCTIC SATURNIID)

Green ghost of night,
with pale purple trails
and long curving tails,
a lover's eyes upon your wings.
You flit among persimmon trees
and ancient stands of hickories.
No mouth to eat
or life to feed—
a pheromone your lure
and one Desire.
She waits—
and will not fly
until you brush her with your feathered crown
and couple her for hours
under the Moon and Saturn,
among the sweet persimmon trees
and ancient stands of hickories,
the deep and leafy dark
that hides her limpid,
silky Beauty.

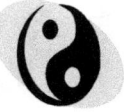

DEER CREEK AT HALLOWE'EN

Vultures wheel in a keening wind
through a leaden sky
to a carcass rot with sin—
resurrection's lie.

Rain has come as nectar sweet
dripping down the leaves;
gone is all of summer's heat,
gone are autumn's sheaves.

A spider scampers through the loam,
a lantern on its back;
white caps whip the lake to foam,
a kitten cries in lack.

Hallowed is the morning light,
hallowed are the trees.
Hallowed is the shoreline's bight,
hallowed are our deeds.

Tease me not with who is best,
grant me leave to nurture.
Rock me with a gentle rest,
soothe me with the future.

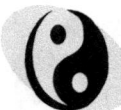

VULNERABILITY

O ancient vulnerability—
the road that I've been on—
a blessed hill ahead of me,
a minotaur behind.
A road of broken pledges
and blighted troths not earned;
occasional oases,
uncommon lessons learned.
And only now I realize
as the way goes on and through,
that each step, stop, and struggle
was a pilgrimage to you.

O sweetest vulnerability,
this place you've let me in;
A deep and hidden sacristy,
well-guarded, and impinged.
Long vanquished and recused—
reclusive and unsung—
last touched by death of one so dear
and moated up against the fear
of dread recurring loss.
And yet I'm here.
You've let me in—
a courageous covenant.
I step through as an avatar
who wields the sword of loving care
and fierce in my complete resolve
to guard the jewel there.
Full girded with a shield
of shared concern and holy trust

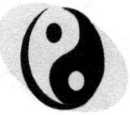

VULNERABILITY
CONTINUED

and bathed in the blue halo
that has engendered us.

By my heart
By my soul
By my head—
Entrusted.

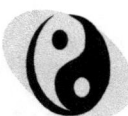

YIN AND YANG AT PLAY

Yin plays soft.
So soft she plays—
soothes, takes in,
gently stays,
droops above his rounded face.
She steps back as he steps in—
Yin dances,
      balances.

Yang plays hard.
      So hard he plays—
      challenges,
      pushes out
      his plans,
      his stands,
thrusting up his face to hers.
As she steps back,
            he steps in.
      Yang prances,
      balances.

His end, her beginning
      her stop, his start.
His light, her dark,
      her cold, his warmth.
His tears, her joy,
      her fears, his ploys.
            Yin and Yang at play.

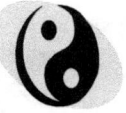

A SACRED PLACE
(DEER CREEK REDUX)

We laud this place as sacred:
a cabin, on a lake.
The sun gilding the water
with winter coming late.

Gossamer and lucent,
insects fly and fall.
A wren incants its blessing;
the trees rise stark and tall.

The sandy prints of buck and doe
prance along the shore;
we follow where the heron stalked,
the water's edge a lure.

We walk—with hearts and hands entwined
and join the evening's trance.
We laud this time as sacred—
a universal dance:

Dance of death and promise,
dance of rise and fall.
Dance of light and darkness,
dance of one, and All.

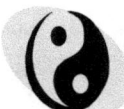

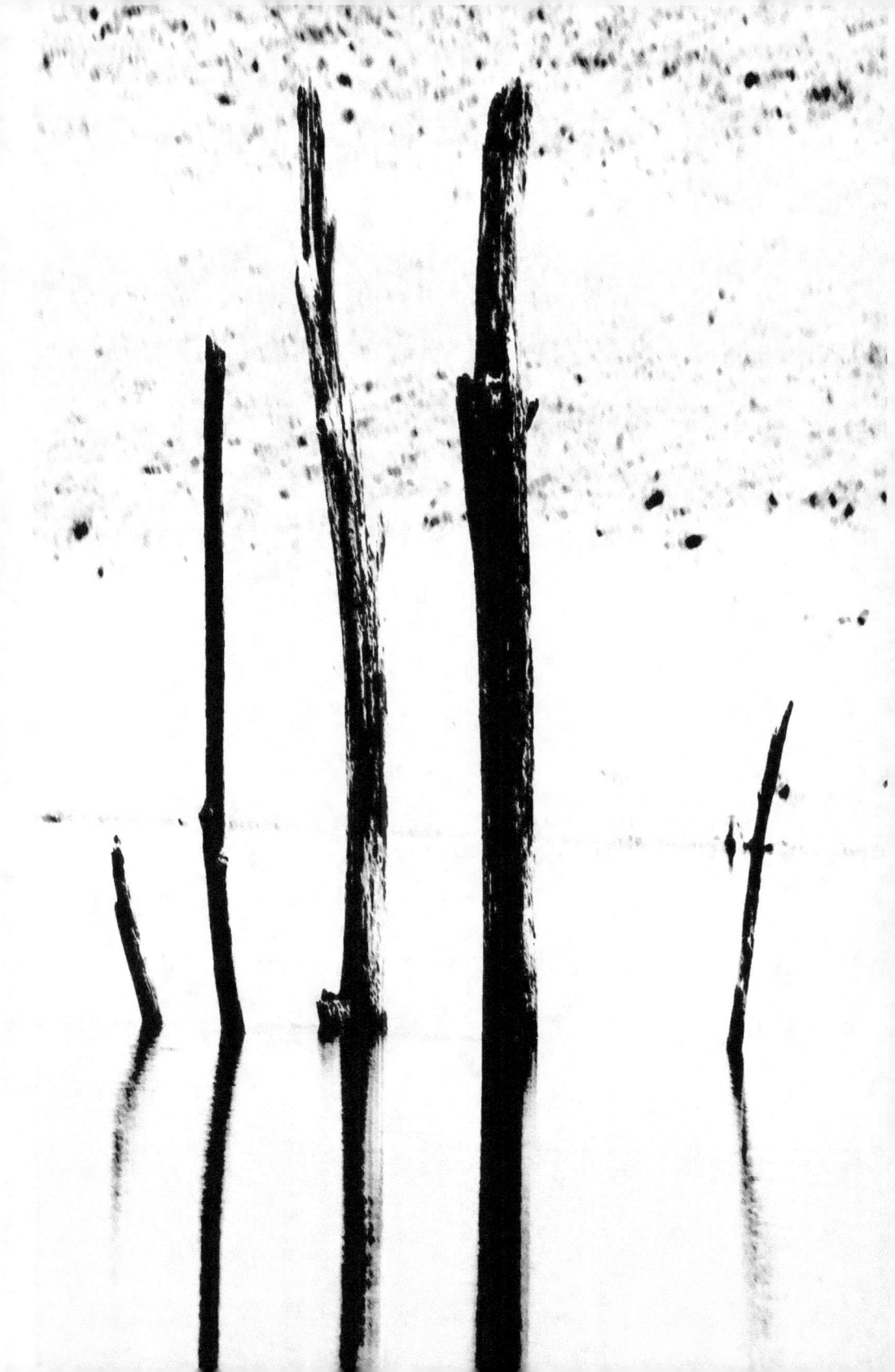

THE HAND OF NIMUE
PHOTO BY PATRICIA THRUSHART

DRINK

Drink me, lover, like a cup
of troth and liquid fealty.

Drink me, darling, like a stream
of sweet and running honey mead.

Drink, oh drink me not just with
thine eyes or mouth or teeth or tongue,
but with a heart's fidelity.

Drink—my salt and sweat
and tears and blood
combine like wine in Oak
or brandied pears of nectar sweet
for you to drink
and drink.

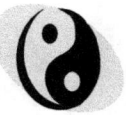

DEPARTURE

A fine mist steals across the lake;
A blackbird calls in disbelief.
Wisps of clouds drift slight and sheer—
your taillights disappear.

The autumn wind stirs barren trees;
The sun lists low and southerly.
Silence falls to mark the end
of Time spent in arrears.

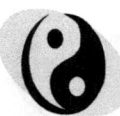

QUANTUM STRINGS

Quantum strings vibrate unseen—
Harmony unheard.
Electrons exist in a cloud
altered at a word.
Schrödinger's Cat lives and dies,
heartbeat undetected.
Particles pass right through our minds
ripples unremembered.

My heart travels point to point,
future state unknown.
The past a cloud of observed states,
The present cast in stone.

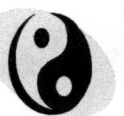

LUNACY

The moon's heart is a wailing Loon—
She pads across the inky lake
Ringed by pine,
Brushed by tangled grasses.
She sounds her haunted manic call
Crazed by Dark
Dazed by Cold—
　　　Lonely.

The moon's soul is a hairy Wolf—
He stalks the frozen winter wood
Filled with snow
Fringed in icy branches.
He lifts his head to howl at her
Crazed by Dark
Dazed by Cold—
　　　Hungry.

A Loon by Day
A Wolf by Dark
The Moon above—
　　　Distant.

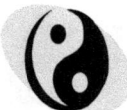

TRUTH

The winnowing hand
rips
now ripe wheat
from once protecting chaff—
no longer needed.

The laser precise
slices
broken DNA
from once programmed genes—
no longer producing.

The hard smooth staff
splits
a sea of red—
fish from weed
shell from rock
pearl from bone.
Alone
a bright Angel
stands
terrible and true.
Unflinching eyes
that look
on what is verily
You.

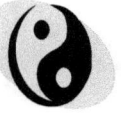

SOLSTICE

I would grow old along with you—
old as pipe and minstrel play
old as hearth and pots of clay
old as red on holly bright
or silver hair in candlelight
or mead in wine
at solstice time
old as logs of first-growth pine
arched across the place we dined
filled with comfort
and Joy.

Gateway Lodge
Cookburg, Pennsylvania
December, 2009

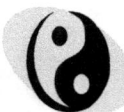

NOVEMBER 28TH

I rise up with the harvest moon,
I rise with yeast and flour.
I rise with voices softly joined
     to grace the dinner hour.

Find me in the sheaves of wheat,
     find me in the snowfall.
Find me in the hunter's woods
     with trees grown bare and tall.

Know that I am with you,
     and give Thanks.

November, 2009

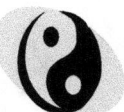

TUCK ME IN

Tuck me in so gently,
Stranger,
come and tuck me in.
Wrap my weary body
round in down
and linen fine.
Down, the down-down-derry
Comfort filled with feathers plucked
black and dense and dreamless
from the Raven's brooding breast.
Linen, woven creamy
as the shroud that once was pressed
to a holy, handsome, dark and lonely haunted
face.
Tuck me in so gently now
and bolster me with clouds.
Let me float above the rain and tears
that do flow down.
Down the down-down-derry down
to join the rushing stream
that joins a thousand rivers
to the ocean of my dreams.
Tuck me in right gently,
Stranger,
come and tuck me in.
Sing to me your songs of joy and peace
Forever-more.

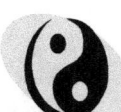

JUNKANOO

I think people who travel can be divided into two camps. Camp One houses those travelers who conduct exhaustive research after buying every published guide for their destination (even packing these guides in spite of their bulk, marked diligently with post-it notes and highlighter pens); who dutifully study the basic greetings in the native language well in advance; who spend months on the internet searching for "inside" information about the things locals do (heaven forbid they should inadvertently act like a tourist); and who choose their travel dates around key events like Mardi Gras, or obscure pilgrimages, or the arrival of the Ruddy Turnstone on the beaches of New Jersey.

Then there is Camp Two, peopled by those who do nothing more than buy their airline ticket for a random date, book a hotel (based on proximity, travel award points, alphabetical order, or dart board) and show up.

I am normally, firmly and unabashedly a member of Camp One. But for a recent trip to Nassau at New Year's, I found myself in the scary, spontaneous and unpredictable "other" Camp. I didn't even research THE WEATHER. I just threw a bunch of summer clothes into a large suitcase and showed up at the airport.

Here is the great life lesson: It made no difference. In fact, not knowing *anything* made *everything* a wonderful surprise.

Take Junkanoo, for instance. Since I had

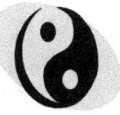

not done my usual "due diligence," I had no idea that on Boxing Day (December 26th) and on New Year's Eve, the wonderful people of the Bahamas throw their hearts and creative spirit into a parade. Well, calling what they do a parade is like calling Carnival in Rio a stroll down the beach. Junkanoo is an art form and a political statement.

Beginning sometime after midnight, and continuing well into New Year's Day morning, the people transform into glittering, pulsing musical beings surrounding floats depicting fantastical creatures of the sea and air. The sounds of whistles, cow bells, and drums become the language of the night.

Or at least that's how it seemed to me the next morning. I didn't plan ahead, and so I didn't buy tickets to sit on the hard metal bleachers lining Bay Street all night; I didn't join the throngs to see the "A" teams rushing to win the grand prizes; I missed the rowdiness, the frenzy, the climax. I spent a quiet New Year's Eve with sand and Caribbean salt water lapping my feet as I drank champagne in a beach chair and a watched a group of German teenagers smoke pot upwind.

But the next morning, I walked out to find the parade was still going on—although winding down. The last of the groups were casually lining up a stone's throw from me. The bleachers were mostly empty, and throngs of Bahamians had begun to sweep the streets. I still managed to collect some souvenirs. . . a white feather tipped in orange, golden trim with rhinestones of blue, a coin, a beer cap.

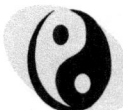

Like fish bones, the skeletons of the great floats—a boat, a bird—lay discarded in parking lots, the crepe paper and feathers torn off. Tired performers dragged their headdresses behind them as they made their way for home, and probably church services. (The Bahamians seemed to be very devoted people). They looked like bower birds, and I a drab sparrow in my khaki. I finally made my way back to the hotel—feeling that I had experienced Junkanoo in a way I couldn't have planned and wouldn't have missed.

I also brought back the next three poems from The Bahamas. I hope you can feel the place as I did. Please consider a visit there someday.

And those free little mementos I picked up? These will grace a shadow box I will make to remind myself of the beauty of Spontaneity.

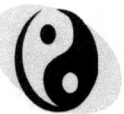

A NASSAU NEW YEAR

A dove coos from shivering palms,
    a ring around her neck.
A moon blue gilds the shore,
    a ring around her breast.
The year new is entered in
      with ringing of the bells
      from austere spires that rise above
      the pink and yellow brick.
Junkanoo parades the street
      with cowbell clangs and whistles;
Lovers pass the jeweled displays
      of rings with diamonds glistened.
My fingers, bare of ring or paint,
      are laced around a glass.
Rings of smoke drift down the beach
      from knots of revelers.
So ring it in—
      this bright new year,
      this rare blue moon,
      this sweet good cheer.
Ring it in—
      the island's charm,
      the people's warmth,
      the sea's green calm.
Ring it in—
      and start to plan
      the next blest time
      in Nassau land.

Nassau, New Providence Island,
Commonwealth of The Bahamas
December 31, 2009

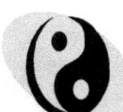

BEFORE OR SINCE

What say you, stranger,
as you drive
your fare across the bay?
"I lost my granny years ago—
a woman unlike any other.
Nineteen ninety one it was—
she made such pretty dresses
and paid for me to go to school
from her dressmaker wages.
'Alfred—marry!' she begged me
while on her bed to die.
I did—
and seven children live
to laud her memory.
This tear that travels down my cheek
is hers and hers alone.
I miss her still.
Her picture—here—don't you see
a woman unlike any other?
Before or since,
before or since.
A woman unlike any other.
Forgive me for my memory,
forgive this little bottle.
Forgive my tears
and bless you now,
Bahaman visitor."

Nassau, New Providence Island,
Commonwealth of The Bahamas
January, 2010

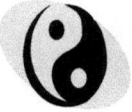

HALL OF WATER

Lost city found
now overrun
now swarmed
by streams of people
spilling down stairs
across blue landings
through green hallways
that echo back
their idle chatter
slot machines
and sandaled patter.
Mouths agape and lungs filled,
small ones dart guppy-like
large ones fart grunty-like
sleek ones cruise sharky-like
and oh—the pretty shiny ones
show their colors angel-like!
Singly or in little groups
they prance along the Plexiglas
watched and marveled at, no doubt,
by all the lovely fishes there.

Atlantis, Paradise Island,
Commonwealth of The Bahamas
January, 2010

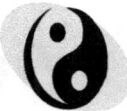

HILDEGARD

Canto 1: PROLOGUE
O sweet voice of the greenest branch
O hands of firmest healing
O heart consumed by living fire
O siren of Sophia
Sealed within the hermit's cave
Before the age of seven
Teacher of both Pope and King
At seventy and seven.

O viridissima virga, ave!

Canto 2: THE CHILD, TITHE
In a predawn twilight
She lies half asleep.
Horses outside snorting,
dampness inside creeps.
Sisters snoring, Mother sobs,
Father pries her from the bed.
With not a word, not a sound,
Snowfall blunts the trotting hooves.
The Abbey spires loom ahead,
One small cell juts at its side.
A thin bright figure—beaming eyes—
Pulls her through the gaping hole.
Monks in brown fall behind as spackles
Make a scraping sound and Light
From sunrise is bricked up.
Her Family gone—forever.

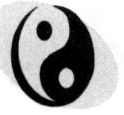

Canto 3: THE GIRL, CLAUSURA
Is it morning?
Is it night?
Is it Montag?
Is It spring?
Visions crowd
Her tender head
Candles sputter
With her breath
Jutta's hands
Are soft and fine
Voices sweet
Are intertwined
Together.

Canto 4: INTERLUDE
O fertile womb now closed and bare
O virgin of the Savior
O visionary of the Egg
O sage of herb and flower
Writer of odd verse and chant
Author of cold wisdom
Artist of the gilded page
Victim of God's calling.

O viridissima virga, ave!

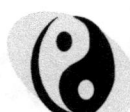

HILDEGARD
CONTINUED

Canto 5: THE WOMAN, ABBESS
Bold and brave
Defying fear
Fierce in vision
Weak in bone
Take your charges
Young and soft
Out from care and safety.

Canto 6: POSTLUDE
Perhaps at Terce or Nones they sing
Perhaps the Angelus
Chant your verse and tend your plot
Filled with leaf and seed.
Fruit that soothes the injured
And demented at your gate.
The Portal green that marks the path
Of blest resilience.

O viridissima virga, ave!

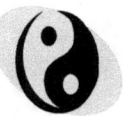

WELHIK-HENY

How the River Became

*When the world was new, a single drop fell from a
green fern leaf. It had started as a tear from the
eyes of a young woman. She loved a strong broad
man, respected in the tribe and feared by his
enemies.*

I sing the Allegheny
Her broad and lovely flanks
Sometimes lush, or laced with snow
That tumbles down her banks

*But he was restless and hungry for more – more
respect, more fear, more love. And so he
wandered, meandered, each day going further
and further, now drifting north, then turning
south. As her tears flowed they followed him, first
as a trickle, then as a stream, then as a
broad and flowing River.*

Born in the plateau highlands
Birthed by secret springs
Fed by every summer rain
Brushed by swallows' wings

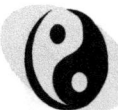

WELHIK-HENY
CONTINUED

Where he turned, and thought of home, a little
tributary appeared: Kiskiminetas, Conewango,
Pucketa. But his turning thoughts did not
last, and still urged on by his desire for more, he
wandered. And so, her tears followed him—now
a great and coursing flood.

Sung to by the Seneca,
Algonquin, pioneer—
Her green and glassy tresses
Her sweet mist rising near

And after a great many miles driven by his lust he
came to a place of confluence, where great waters
flowed together—those of his woman's tears, and
those of the children she would never have with
him; those of the grandchildren who would never
honor him; those of his mother who had lost him;
those of his grandmothers who mourned him.

She shelters river otters
And spawns the spring mayfly
Herons step and poke her mud
For frogs and small walleye

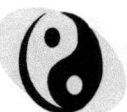

WELHIK-HENY
CONTINUED

*And in this great confluence, his foolish strength
was overcome, and he sank below the green and
glassy surface. He sank to the silky bottom and
tumbled, eye to eye with the walleye and musky.
He tumbled and was drawn out over leagues and
time, until he himself was made a fish, with gills
and scales, with no voice and no tears. Through
the Ohio he swam, through the Mississippi until
he came to the great Mouth.*

I drove her length and mile
One solemn winter day
Along man's concrete rivers
With signs that bear her name

*And there he was spit out, and lost to his native
land, in a great and strange expanse of water
where no power, no love and no fear was
found. His family cried for him, and to this day,
feed the lovely Allegheny with their sadness and
lost memory.*

66

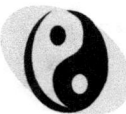

WELHIK-HENY
CONTINUED

Across her graceful course
The hemlock and the maple
Bend to her like lovers
And touch if they are able

I sing the Allegheny
And she sings back to me
Her chant of river riches
Her scent of memory.

Welhik-heny.

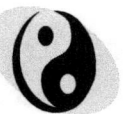

BIRCH-NESS

She stands amid a barren clan
still clothed
and yet she shivers
with every wisp of winter wind
she quivers
and whispers
dry and golden secrets
from her rooted soul
of birds that fledged or insect galls
that mauled
her woody memory.
As her spicy sap unfolds
she furls
the green of spring
in little whorls
to welcome slanted light
and longer days.
A slender thing
with limbs askance
no child will climb up—
no tree house hammered
to her skin—
no rope swing—
or other thing
like oaks endure.
But she in all her tenderness
is at the once
both tensile
and sure.

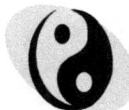

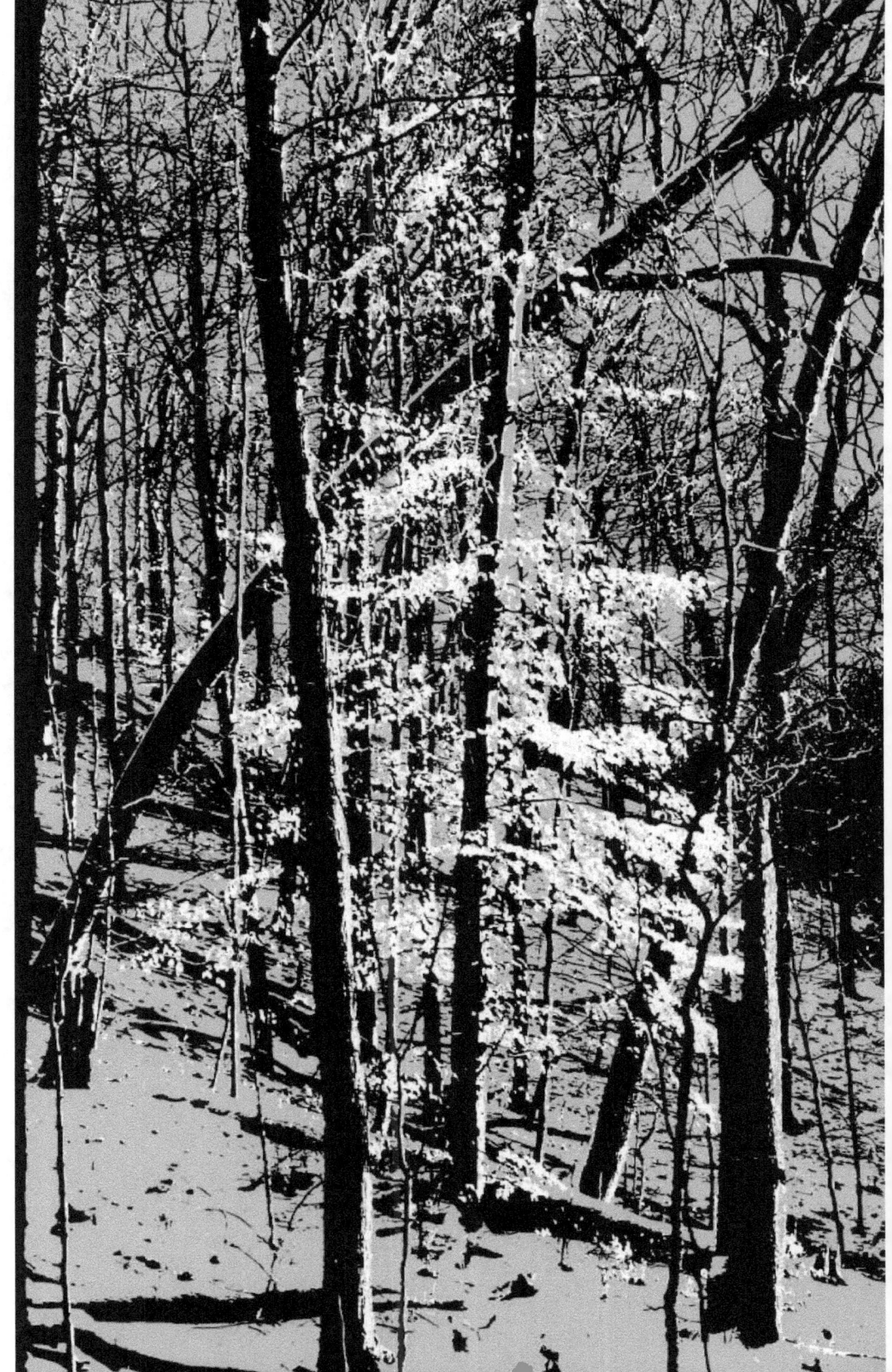

AMID THE BARREN CLAN
PHOTO BY PATRICIA THRUSHART

RACE FOR THE CURE

In May of 2010, I kept a very important promise to my sister.

On the day she was diagnosed with breast cancer, I made a promise to her that she would walk with me and our girls, cancer-free, in the next Komen Race for the Cure® . At the time, I really didn't know if fate and medical science would allow us to keep this promise. Her prognosis was uncertain; her treatment of chemotherapy and radiation loomed before her. I made the promise firmly and with a certainty I did not feel. I made it to encourage her, to uplift her, to give her strength.

I made it with fingers crossed and candles lit.

Nearly a year later, and with great joy, we kept the promise. We formed a team, "Rachel's Friends," to participate in the Race which is held every Mother's Day in Schenley Park, Pittsburgh. Our mother, daughter, nieces, and friends joined. We solicited contributions which, according to the Foundation, "fund local innovative outreach, awareness and treatment programs for the medically underserved throughout Western and Central Pennsylvania as well as national cutting-edge breast cancer research." With the generosity of friends and family, "Rachel's Friends" outpaced its fundraising goals almost immediately.

As I write this, my sister has emerged from her battle with this terrible disease. Her

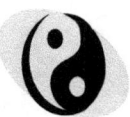

hair has grown back (and more beautiful than ever!), her skin has recovered its luster, her eyes shine with hope and confidence for the future. Her genetic tests were negative— which means our girls do not face an increased risk. But we all have some risk. One in eight women hear this diagnosis; and not all are as lucky as my sister. Hers was diagnosed early— through a routine mammogram— treated swiftly and conquered successfully. Her tumor was receptive to estrogen-based drug therapy. But at the Race, many participate *in memoriam,* not *in celebration*.

Forty thousand people walk or run in the Race in Pittsburgh. Many more are impacted by this disease in this moderate-sized city.

My dear friend, if you are a woman, get your mammogram regularly as recommended by your health professional. Early detection is critical. If you are a man, insist that every woman you love do the same. And if there is a charity event to support the Susan B. Komen Foundation in your area, participate!

While tremendous advances have been made to fight this disease, the real frontier is prevention. One in eight women, friends!

One in eight.

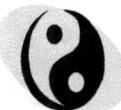

A MAN
WHO WOULD GROW OLD

You are a man who would grow old
with every graying hair
or deepened crease
or slack of skin—
rejecting creams or dyes
or wiles—
oh you rejoice
and smooth your bangs
and why?
Your father died—
did not grow old
did not grow white
did not grow thin on top—
He Stopped
(his precious breath and heart and thought).
Robbed of age
he froze in time
at forty-nine
(a handsome man)
and so
you celebrate each change
each passing year
each new blank page
as you approach
the age he Passed—
as if a precious Gift:
You are a man who would grow old
in the fullness of Joy.

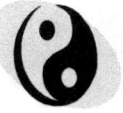

HE MOVES
UPON THE WATER

He moves upon the water,
      across The Lake of Souls
      with those who dive down deep to duck
      His life-commanding Hand.
Wrestled like the angel
      in Jacob's restless dream;
      burning bright upon a bush to alter
      Moses' face.
Elijah hides within a cloak to block His
      whispered call—
      and hides from—
      Change.
Our Nemesis
      and constant supplicant
      whom we embrace
      or run from hard depending on our Fate.
One moment kind—as Fortunes grow,
      or Love ignites our Heart,
      but at the next, so Heartless, as death
      demands its due,
      or illness stalks our frailest Peace—
      of Mind.
Like Acts of God,
      which rob us of our daily fool's belief
      in Status Quo:
The human prayer for life and true divinity.

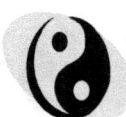

BLIZZARD

On this the day that
      Winter made
      do you rejoice in it?
The deep cold snow
      the temperature low—
      do you rejoice in it?
With power gone
      and candles lit
      do you rejoice in it?
The car snowed in
      and Walmart closed—
      do you rejoice in this?
No Facebook, e-mail, internet-
      do you rejoice in it?
Are books true friends?
Are pets true loves?
Are you your best companion?
If so—
      may you rejoice
      and be glad
      in that.

On February 7, 2010, Pittsburgh Pennsylvania received 20
inches of snow

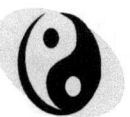

FEBRUARY

A small bird calls as I walk out
    this cold and dawning day
    (white and gray—
    ice and ash
        with red upon his chest)
He Chants:
    peter-peter-peter
    (Rock of Christ)
    peter-peter-peter
    (the bedrock crucified)
A song of sacrifice
    and abstinence
    of lent and self denial
The expiated sun;
    no greening branch
    or budding bush
    or early crocus stem.

He sings.

The World is all encased in ice
    that snow alone has cleansed.
        Crystalline,
    cold as sin—
    and ash, his birthmark,
        forever upon his crest.

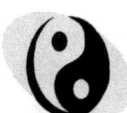

THE MOON WILL BE MY WEDDING RING

The moon will be my wedding ring—
    scimitar and sickle—
    horns wrapped 'round my
    knuckle white,
    earthshine-glazed and winkled.
Cast in cherry-blossom spring,
    bridesmaid-pink and petaled;
    evenstars on left and right
    of diamond planet pendants.
I am adorned,
    adored,
    and hoard
    my lover's beaming rhymes
    upon the starry evening's breath
    and night-time's whispered climes.
A marriage band once torn from earth,
    mined by the crash of planets
    that stumbled in their perfect dance
    with carbon-crystal comets.
The moon will grace my wedding night—
    lunula and crescent—
    wrapped around my knuckle white
    and wrists of vein and marble.
And I will dance—
    my husband's forehead
    pressed against my brow—
    the moon a glistening promise
    the sky a concave vow.

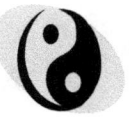

SPRING

Spring
      is early
      and
      in the secret
      vernal places
      rain collects
      in ponds—
      those spaces
      once brittle-dry
      so frogs can sing.
We turn
      with our diurnal souls
      and face the Sun
      so that our hearts
      can bloom
      with sweet spring beauties
      and blush
      all at once
      with tender shoots of
      unfurling
      Bloodroot.

Deer Creek
April 1, 2010

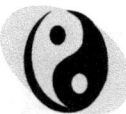

LARK

Lark—
Rise up!
From mists of memory
     and fallow meadows—
Lark Arise!
Emboldened,
     chest emblazoned
     in yellow-gold and black—
     the victor's splendor marked there—
Arise!
I hear your song
     from far afield
     in drowsy morning dreams—
     out of place
     and out of time.
You call me back,
     my lover's arms around me.
"A lark'" he says—
"A Meadowlark"—
     just as my memory claims you
     and begs you to Arise!

Deer Creek
Easter Sunday, 2010

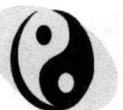

DEMONS STALK US BOTH, MY TROTH

Demons stalk us both, my troth—
we are so much beloved by them
   Our neural fire
   our shining eyes
   our gifts of thought
   and time and rhyme
Rise up in them
a jealous blood
and stir them to
the haunt.

Yours are from the past, my sweet—
they visit ruthlessly
to wake your sleep
or walk with you
as you return
to where you would but weep
   Beside a grave
   or by a stream
   or at the precipice
and in each place you looked to find
some love or tolerance
or fate
but where you found, too late,
for naught
you fought—
caught in the dance of yes and no
where hearts hang off the hook.

They will not let you forget.

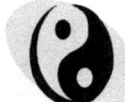

DEMONS STALK US BOTH, MY TROTH
CONTINUED

And mine are from the future, love—
they threaten growing old
    the loss of hair
    the loss of care
    with every spot or crease;
the drying up, the tearing down—
desiccate and fading.
They ply their wares
bewildering
of scalpel, cream and needle
admonishing "you can't grow old
without a fight"—
judged on sight
in conference rooms and parties.

They will not let me accept.

And so we cling—
and sing
and love
we laugh
and look for beauty rare—
and when our demons ask their due
we cry
and help each other
pay the price unfair.
We will not let them triumph.

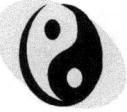

SYCAMORE

Ghostly, through a hemlock stand
beside an icy stream
mottle-blanched
brittle-branched,
limbs raised bleached
and swaying--
　　　"Sick I am,
　　　 sick I am,
　　　 sick I am for love."

Moonlit, in a timbered land
below a vaulted ridge
rattle-dry
rasped-cry
peeling down
and weeping—
　　　"No nest have I,
　　　 no rustled bray
　　　 or tufted owlet sleeping,

　　　 Oh sick am I,
　　　 sick am I,
　　　 sick am I with love."

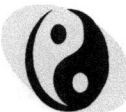

FOR LAUREN

I call you forth
Beauty
forth from your crystal tomb
healed and whole
with wings unfurled
throbbing bright
vein etched
and ready
to thrust you up
aloft
a-flight
a wondrous sight
above the cares of what is done
up toward the Sun
that soaks your weary body through
with pulse and new resilience.
And thus engorged
and thus engaged
your supple wings
extend their reach
and bid you now to
Soar.

Dedicated to a young woman battling cancer

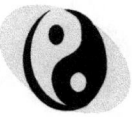

STARQUAKE

Starquake
    oscillate
        roil across a sun's face
    boil a storm
          that arcs to space
    so dark and cold
and waiting

Earthquake
    rocks shake
        grind across tectonic plates
    shifting hard
         intractable weight
    so blind and strong
and stubborn

Moonquake
    sun-baked
        ripple through a dry lake
    dust of comets
          stirs awake
    so dry and fine
and fleeting

Man quakes
    in wonder
        at the thought—
          we are
    the stuff
        of stars

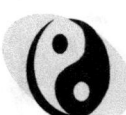

GRANT'S TOMB

"Who is buried in Grant's tomb"?
An old joke often spoke
  before another grim and granite
  gray facade along another
  broad and greening gauntlet.
Asked of children, mostly
  as they pause bunched up closely
  heads stuffed full of all
  the laws and dates and facts
  that craft their birthright sovereignty.
Who is buried in Grant's tomb?
  Tired kids will fall for it and answer
  "I don't know!"
  and some adults do too.
So—who is buried in Grant's tomb?
A friend, a man, a mentor?
A Casanova with a trail
  of pussy cats like the Pied Piper?
  Or someone, somehow less than this.
Ordinary.
Fighting his Ulyssian foes
  of jealousy, suspicion of inadequacy
  and very likely—Boredom.
Full met on the golf battlefield
  with guile and Trojan Horses
  and all the while
  wishing that he
  was somehow more
  like you.

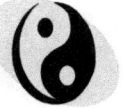

BELTANE

I am come into the greenwood
    all on the first of May
    to nestle in my lover's bower
    built upon the boughs and flowers
    he has laid for me.
His maypole is erected,
    planted firm in silken moss,
    adorned with ribbon from my hair
    and dewdrops trembling in the fair
    sun that gilds the clearing.
He beckons me
    and I, his Flora,
    rush to his embrace—
    his eyes like woodland violets
    his mouth sweet with the taste
    of seed and nectar.
We kiss—
    and summer's promise
    bursts upon my brow:
    the fruits of vine and branch,
    the bloom of Maia's vow.

May 1, 2010

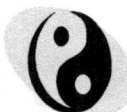

THE FACIAL

I feel
> my skull beneath the skin
> thin
> and brittle
> as her facile hands
> massage with mask and cream.

I dream
> of high cheekbones and deep eye-sockets
> hollow temples, interlocked
> with joints now holding jaw to bone.
> Alone

I rest
> under the sheets
> that drape, shroud-like
> caress cloud-like
> and clearly, suddenly, I see
> my skeleton
> white and diaphanous and dry.

Delicate, it lies
> intact on a steel table
> while men of science—from the future—
> lean above with gloves and sutures,
> probing tools
> and brilliant lights
> and follow clues
> with storied whispers
> to reconstruct

My flesh.

May, 2010

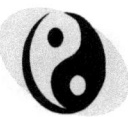

87

CREATIVITY

In the beginning, when God created the heavens and the earth, the earth was a formless wasteland, and darkness covered the abyss.
—The New American Bible

The creation of something new is not accomplished by the intellect but by the play instinct acting from inner necessity. The creative mind plays with the objects it loves.
—Carl Jung

My daughter and I went to play, as Jung would have it— we went to a local pottery place to express our creativity. Actually I had a need. I wanted to make a tile that said "Dishwasher Dirty" to put in the sink as a reminder to my two teenagers to put their dirty dishes in said dishwasher instead of said sink. A very utilitarian outcome for an afternoon of creative expression! But I had also brought my book of poetry, "Little Girl Against The Wall", in case I felt inspired to use my own text on a mug or bowl or dish.

Walking in, I saw a former business colleague sitting at the table with her girlfriend, Constance. It had been years since we worked together, so I reintroduced myself and we started talking about creativity—and the importance of keeping in touch with one's inner play instinct (how Jungian) while working in the very analytical and numbers-oriented world of

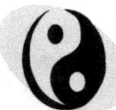

financial services. I mentioned my poetry, and my ongoing struggle to define myself as "something" so creative as a Poet. We talked about balancing work and life, and the richness that creative expression brings to life. Her girlfriend, it turns out, is the only full-time employee of a charitable organization that helps women transition from welfare into the working world. Before I had painted a single dot, I had given them my book, and agreed to be a speaker at an upcoming meeting of her charity's professional woman's group.

We each retreated into our choices of color, intensity and design; and our frustrations with brushes, stamps and the gap between the object beheld in the mind's eye, and the object glistening on the paper-covered table. Before long my tile was done and fired, picked up and doing its duty in the sink. (My teenagers, of course, ignored it completely.) I had almost forgotten the conversation about doing a presentation on life balance and creative expression when I received an e-mail from Constance asking if I was available on a certain date to address her organization's clients and volunteers.

Oh panic! I had stood before hundreds of people to give presentations on topics in my field, to announce organizational changes to my employees, and even to sing a program of early music. In fact I am one of the very few people who actually enjoy public speaking. But never had I the temerity to stand up as a Poet. This was a big step. A very big step.

I said yes.

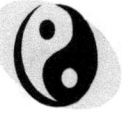

And so a few months later I found myself, after a long day of work, walking to the building where the group was to meet. I had brought along another copy of my book to read from and to raffle off. I did not bring:

1) a power point presentation

2) index cards with prepared remarks, or

3) an outline, memorized from many practice sessions, of my presentation.

I had decided to speak spontaneously, extemporaneously and from the heart. *And I was very nervous about that.*

It was the first time I was unsure of my credentials as a public speaker.

The small room was full when I entered, and after a very short preamble, Constance introduced me. It was a small group, and so we could afford the time to have each person talk about what she hoped to get from our discussion.

It was tremendously inspiring to me as I could glimpse the challenges and determination these women felt.

I stood up in my business suit and pumps and for the first time, did not invoke the "C-level" professional with a Master's Degree.

I found the voice of the poet!

Oh, we talked about balancing work and life, and the need to stay in touch with the inner child at play, and the "value" that such skills might bring to an employer. But for most of the time, I read my poetry.

I was astounded at the reaction.

There were tears.

There were sighs.

There was laughter.

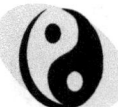

And then, there were questions.

The presentation almost became a joint therapy session fueled by kindness and common experience. For example, all of us seemed to have a lot to forgive in our past.

Not all of us had done so—yet.

All of us had suffered loss of confidence and direction.

Not all of us were back on the forward road—yet.

All of us had faced issues of aging, acceptance by society, and image.

Not all of us were self-accepting—yet.

We all got a little closer to each other, and to these milestones, after this special time together.

When I left the session, drained but exhilarated, the sounds of the raffle chased me down the hall. The winner was actually thrilled to win my book! A rush of emotion, wonder and joy welled up in me. I had seen for myself— and been the agent of— the healing power of poetry shared with good intention.

I have donated many items of clothing to that charitable organization since and have felt much joy imagining these women—the one just starting her first job after years of welfare, the one starting her own business, the one writing a journal, the one still struggling to get on her feet— wearing my clothes, with my poetry in their hearts and my voice in their ears.

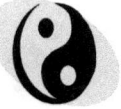

THE DISTANCE

The sprinter's bane
The lover's curse
The soldier's gauntlet
      airline's purse,
      baby's first steps,
      last hearse ride
      bridge's span,
Newfoundland tide.
The fighter's taunt,
      surveyor's tool
NASA's challenge,
      Olympic pool.
Marathon minutes,
      fasting day,
      last home stretch,
      the month of May.

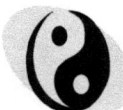

CAT ON MY STOMACH

Cat on my stomach
     (nose-to-nose)
What will you be
     when you cease to be
     this elegant mass of
     muscle and fur—
     this electromagnetic
     neuro-kinetic
     pure cunning
     all hunting machine?
Tooth and claw
     slit-eyed, pad-pawed
     regal, erect—
     and barely kept
     tame
     curled on the soft pillow
     always preferred
     purring and dreaming; yes,
     in a word:
A Cat.
What will you be
     when you cease to be
     my little pet
     taken by age or disease or disaster—
     a misguided chase or injuries after

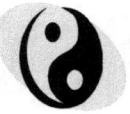

CAT ON MY STOMACH
CONTINUED

     a fall
     after all
     like me, you can't live forever
     except in someone's
sweet, sad
     memory.

For Satchmo aka MoMo or Mr. Mo who died
May 6, 2010

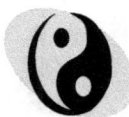

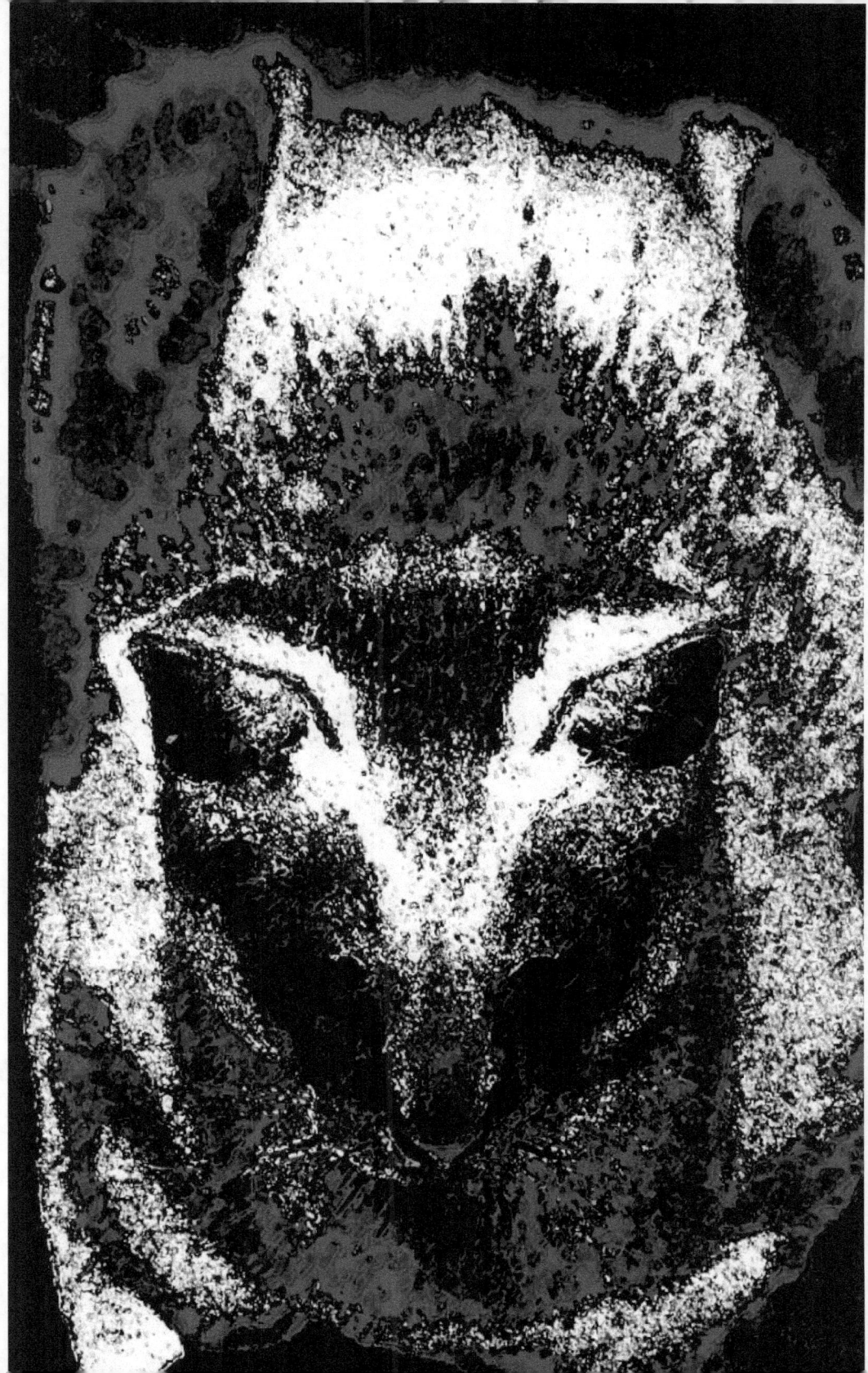

MR. MO
PHOTO BY PATRICIA THRUSHART

BEND, WILLOW, BEND

Bend, willow, bend—
bend and hang low,
trail your leafy fingers
in the River that now flows
past your slender body,
across your rooted toes:
the coursing font of memories
the Present only knows.

Bend, and brush the water
where the setting sunlight sparks
with gleams that seem to dance in Joy
and gild your weathered bark.
Hear the yellow warbler
as he sings his sweeter song
to Lovers that are kneeling there—
your frailest twigs fall in their hair,
your lacy leaves perfume the air
they breathe to pledge their Future.

Bend, willow, bend—
bend and hang low.

June 1, 2010
Allegheny River

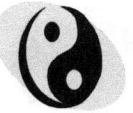

97

ON HEBRON'S HEATH

On Hebron's heath
I drink my spate
of bitter herbs and wormwood
like vinegar upon the stake
with streaks of ash upon my face.
Remember woman thou art dust—
the very dust of stars you love—
and unto dust you will return
far past this looming gauntlet.
So call upon your goddess wild
and rent your sackcloth garments—
Artemis, her vigor full—
call on her to train you.
The arrow cocked,
the bow engaged,
as fleet of foot as Hermes.
Your chastity her great concern,
your fortitude her treasure,
your victory her pleasure. . .

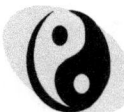

ALCHEMY

I lie awake at night
at times
as women do
(and do you, too?)
and trace the lines of thoughts and dreams
of what I've done
or what to do
or what I seem to be
or see
and just beyond my reverie
there lies a great and deep abyss
pitch dark
and stark: **Nigredo**

Then sweat will bead upon my skin,
clammy cool and alabaster
while my heart beats the faster
and sheaths my body in the dark
so sheets and limbs shine brighter: **Albedo.**

My hair streams red across the bed
where passion's remnants linger
in soft folds swollen, ruby-blushed: **Rubedo.**

The looming dark
the shining skin
the bruised and reddened passion
may without warning crystallize
a gold transformation: **Citrino.**

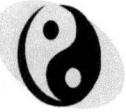

I WILL HAVE
ROSES IN THE WOODS

I will have Roses in the woods,
incongruous and vagrant,
bending over my bare bones,
ponderous and fragrant.
Raining petals on my grave,
blowsy-pink and blatant,
with hips that cause the stems to bow,
thorny-arched and latent.

A thrush will serenade my soul,
breasted red and cheerful;
giving to the dawn its song,
ethereal and blissful.
Bidding that my spirit rise,
insistently and joyful,
to roam the dark and loamy tract,
diaphanous and peaceful.

July, 2010

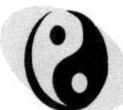

WITNESS

They found a Ship
beneath the Pit—
an 18th Century beauty—
lined with grime,
the sea's salt rime,
bended oak soaked gray with time—
its prow carved high and masthead fixed
to cleave the wild River Styx
and vanquish detestation.

I see it now—
it rises spectral, Viking-proud,
aglow with funeral ash and pyre—
and gathers in its hull the souls
that fell to rift and blast and fire
(they perished there against their Will
and all the Laws of Man).
New walls will stand
but not a single soul is banned
to wander there:
for each has risen—
Faith ablaze—
and travels on through wave and wave
to halls of Truth and Witness.

*On July 15, 2010 The New York Times reported that a
construction crew working at the site of the fallen World
Trade Towers (The Pit) had found the hull of a wooden ship
buried two centuries ago, 20 feet below the current street
level.*

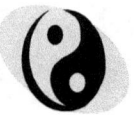

WIND ME UP IN VEILS

Wind me up in veils
      to hide the face of my Conceit.
Shield me, shape me,
      have me shift again—
      a facile feat.
I morph from friend to mother,
      poetess or wife-to-be
      depending on the place and time
      and what I have to manage.
I shift and travel half engaged
      through wormhole after Hour—
Time undone and then repaired,
      Past and Future melded where
      the Truth must suit the Moment.

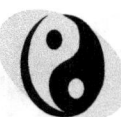

DRESS FOR SUCCESS

I happened on the "Dress for Success" (DFS) booth on the exhibit hall floor during a recent Conference for Women sponsored by the Pennsylvania Governor's office. My fifteen-year-old daughter was with me—and that in and of itself was wonderful. What an experience to share with her! By this time we had already met many of my work colleagues, and heard several inspiring keynote speakers. I was in full "professional banker" mode, suited up in pumps and pantyhose, as we went from booth to booth together. I heard my name called out and turned to see the DFS Executive Director jumping out of her chair, arms open to hug me.

She introduced me to the volunteers at the booth as "the poet who spoke at our Professional Women's Group," and they responded with excitement, like I was a minor celebrity. One, a young woman, pulled me aside to tell me how inspired she was reading my first book, "Little Girl Against The Wall." She pressed her heart as she spoke. As I was attending the Conference as a senior business woman from a New York-based bank, this notoriety as a poet first was amazing to me— and tremendously touching.

You see, in my mind, the selfless determination of these volunteers to help women in the most tactical and meaningful way possible was the greater gift. They immediately solicited me to participate in a video they were making on-site. It only took a few minutes—

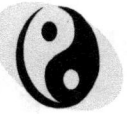

but as my daughter stood by watching, I knew it was a lifetime memory in the making. They asked me what I felt was the key to success, and I responded: Inner Confidence. Such a precious commodity for most women! Few are born with it; this kind of confidence is built up by a certain type of experience that takes us beyond comfort and reticence to confront risk. When a woman does this, she learns her own mettle— and indeed, whether she succeeds or fails is not the point.

So— my message to the video camera, and to my daughter was: *Seek it! Volunteer! Accept the assignment!* Try that new thing, and don't be afraid to fail: *For failure is not the measure and risk is not the foe.*

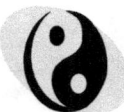

THE UN-DONE NIGHT

Late summer
    after sunset
    and I walk beneath the canopy
    of Sycamore and Maple tree
    and in their leaves and limbs and height
    the insects sing The Night.

Shrill and trill and slight
    they sing of starlight
    blanched by streetlight;
    the fitful shine of Venus,
    the faint red spark of Antares,
    the wistful beam of Deneb
    and the lost jeweled Milky Way.

Shadows cast by stars they sing
    without a voice or larynx
    as fiddlers do;
    they scrape and rub and bow
    with wing and leg and sticky toe
    with thorax, pincer, spike—

They peer through eyes that scatter stars
    across the undone night
To pierce their tiny insect souls
    that pine for ancient light.

And so they sing unceasingly—
    their clicks and thrums increasing
    with a shimmered pulsing might;
    they sing an insect memory
    of spangled starry flight.

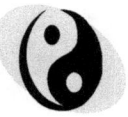

SWALLOW—WING!

Swallow- wing!
Flit-hover-flutter-fly!
Start and dart,
Skim on a whim
In light bright white-breasted
feathered-freedom-flight!
Slight and joyful
Unfettered
Twist and dive: Alive!

Heart-try!
Gravity-grounded
Life-pounded
Mourning-clothed
In business matters,
Career ladders,
Pump-shod, foot-trod,
Worn-torn and once lorn,
Shed these clothes
And with the swallow— Soar!

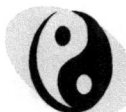

RONNIE FULL WISE

Blue eyes dimmed
    rimmed
    with the dust and
    crust of age—
The twinkled sage
    peers through white
    cataract and cloud,
    full wise from
    oft-survived attacks
    of life out-loud
    and sweet surrendered love.
Demise is soon, no doubt;
    the journey out
    respected
    but not feared.
Oh Death can leer
    but cannot dampen the Joy
    of a seer in her latter years.
Children if ye be brave
    sit here
    spend a moment of your
    spendthrift time
    and Listen.

In memory of Veronica, my beloved maternal grandmother.
October 27, 2010

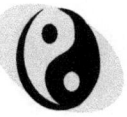

MEASURE

What is the measure of a man?
How is he to be judged?
By bank account,
trust fund amount,
his style of car,
or just how far he travels to the office?
The house he owns,
his type of phone,
the value of his watches;
his girth,
net worth,
his pecs or abs,
or where he went to college?
Or is it all the sons he touched
or daughters he inspired
through truth of love
or love of truth—
his stalwart heart,
his broken dreams,
his fierce fight for the future.

October, 2010

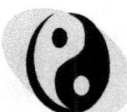

HEARING

To live
        where I can hear
        Nothing
            or Everything
                or Every Little Thing:
Where a honk
        is a goose
            gaggling for its mate
            in a twilight pond
That distant whine
        a bee
            dancing the memory
                of late balm and blossom
That piercing whistle
        a hawk
            tail spread
                red-glinted and broad
That rush of noise
        the wind
        playful and sharp
            this October day
            teasing leaves
                from their sugar-sap homes
                to crackle and crunch
                    as I scruff by
                    in my autumn aural reverie

October, 2010

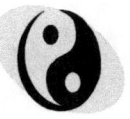

FROSTED FIELDS

There's beauty in the frosted fields
    with haystacks piled high
    the rubbled corn left on the ground
    and winter's fierceness nigh

As skeletons of goldenrod—
    dry sentinels—remain
    to speak of autumn's once-red hue
    to whisper summer's gain

Frost has killed
    and yet the earth sustains
    its chosen kind—
    a fox amid the crusted stalks,
    a hawk above the pines—

The dew collects on weaver's webs
    left ragged, insect-torn,
    and freezes into mandalas
    for spiders yet unborn

November, 2010

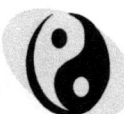

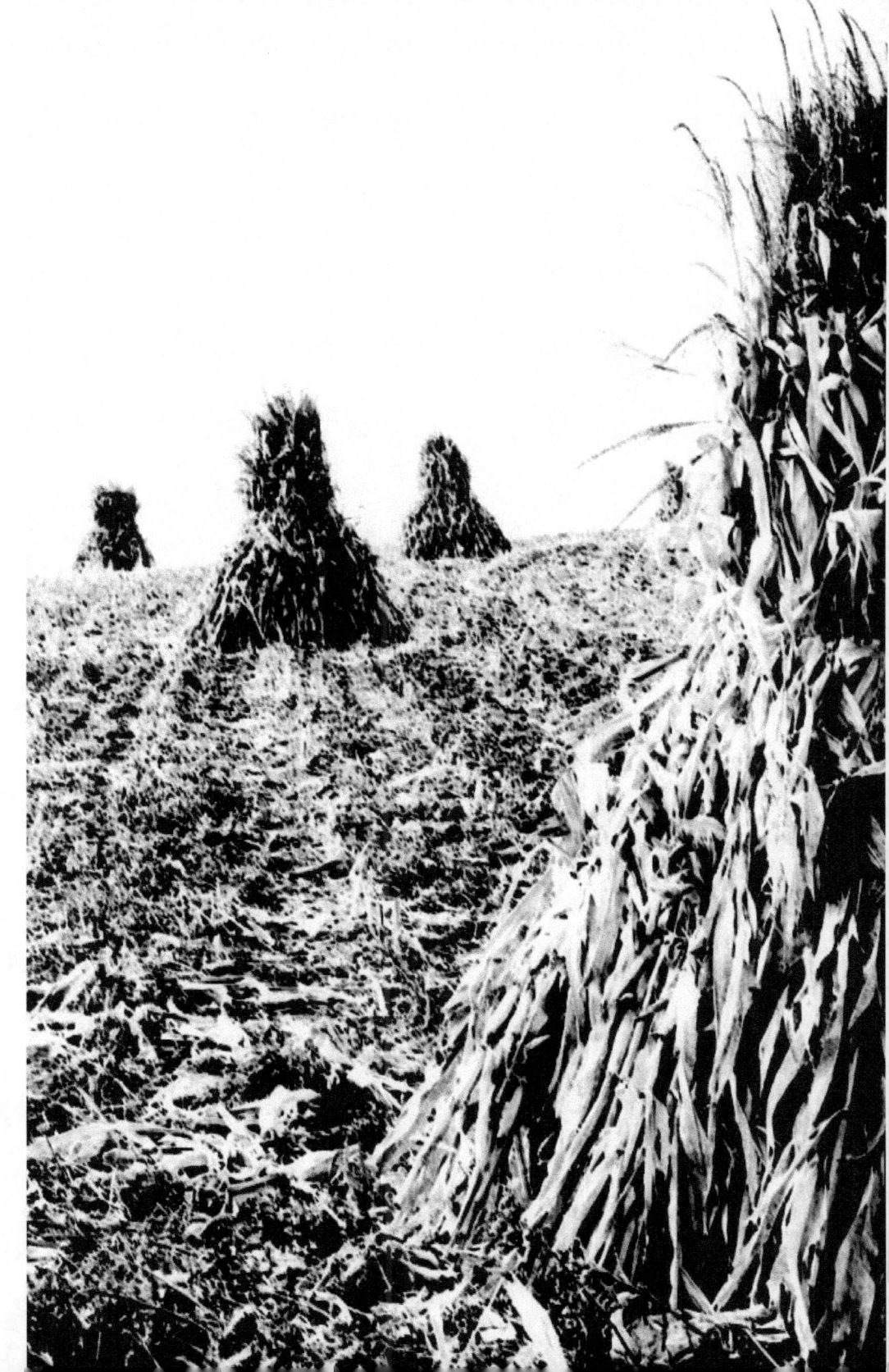

A MURDER OF CROWS*

A covey of quail scatters,
A kettle of hawks soars,
A gaggle of geese vectors, but
A murder of crows grows,
starts slowly, singly,
silently winging a solitary way
across the darkling November day.
A moment later
more swiftly, more fly
until hundreds stream by—
an oil-black river
of bone and feather,
fingered and splayed
and beating their way
to the tree roost of Winter.
A great city of flight
where— rustling, cackling,
fluttering, speckling—
thousands of Corvus will spend the night.
Forgotten now the breeding pair,
dismiss the life-long mate:
the Crows of Winter
Congregate.

But ah, the despair of the people nearby!
The noise, the disease, the waste!

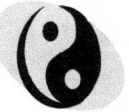

A MURDER OF CROWS
CONTINUED

And so the local council votes
and all concerned agree to smite
these birds well known to mourn their dead:
state-sponsored, hate-mongered,
the humans commission
a wide-scale murder of crows.

A group of crows is called a "murder."
November, 2010

As published in the January 2011 edition of The
Pennsylvania Society for Ornithology newsletter.

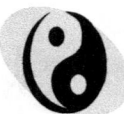

BOOK-END DEDICATION

The Yin-Yang symbol was developed by the ancient Chinese based on the beautiful and insistent dance of the universe in the sky above us. It happens like this: Place a pole in the ground. Over time, note the direction of the sunrise and sunset, and the when the sun casts its shortest and longest shadows. Name these directions East, West, South and North. Call the shortest shadow "Summer Solstice" and the longest "Winter Solstice."

Take a pencil and paper, and draw a circle to represent the sky. Divide it by five concentric circles from the center, and then use radiating lines to divide your circle further into twenty-four segments. Now, painstakingly over one year, mark the length of the shadow of your pole every day. Keep the summer side lighter (more sun). Shade the winter side darker (more moon).

The result: Yin and Yang—the entire celestial dance in one symbol.

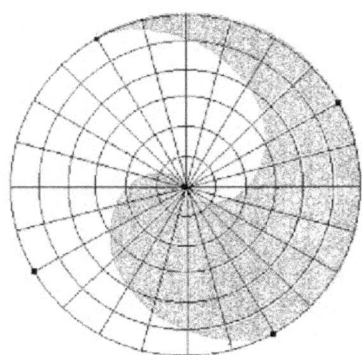

This dance is echoed in every aspect of nature, including human nature. When you find this balance, you find peace. It is my earnest belief that every one of us has this balance inside of us: male and female, strong and weak, outward and inward. It is my earnest wish that you, reader, find and embrace it. If my poems have helped you do that, then I am blessed.

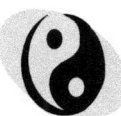

ABOUT THE AUTHOR

Patricia Thrushart is the nom de plume of a woman in her middle years and a mother of two wonderful teenagers. She currently lives in a small neighborhood just outside of Pittsburgh, Pennsylvania. Although neither her Bachelor's degree nor her Master's Degree is in Poetry, it has always been a great love of hers, both as a writer and student. In between poems, she has pursued a career as an executive at a global financial institution.   Most, but not all, of the poetry in this book was written over the past year— a time of great revelation and metamorphosis. As Yin and Yang exert their forces on her life, the biography in her next book is sure to be different. She looks to the future with joy, seeking balance and peace.

Patricia Thrushart

October 2011

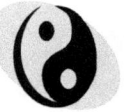

117

PERSONAL NOTES

www.ingramcontent.com/pod-product-compliance
Lightning Source LLC
Chambersburg PA
CBHW072214170526
45158CB00002BA/600